WILL
SMITH

WILL SMITH

Stacey Stauffer

CHELSEA HOUSE PUBLISHERS
Philadelphia

To Dad, Mom, Scott, and "Gram," for the many years of love, laughter, faith, and creative encouragement. And to Shawn for his love and for his generous and immeasurable assistance with this work.

The author gratefully acknowledges the cooperation of Mr. Ronald Matthews and Mr. David Ridgeway of Overbrook High School, who provided personal interviews for this volume.

Chelsea House Publishers

Editor in Chief	Stephen Reginald
Production Manager	Pamela Loos
Managing Editor	James D. Gallagher
Picture Editor	Judy L. Hasday
Art Director	Sara Davis
Senior Production Editor	Lisa Chippendale

Staff for WILL SMITH

Project Editor	James D. Gallagher
Editorial Assistant	Anne Hill
Associate Art Director	Takeshi Takahashi
Designer	Keith Trego
Picture Researcher	Patricia Burns
Cover Illustration	Robert Gerson

The Chelsea House World Wide Web site address is http://www.chelseahouse.com

First Printing

1 3 5 7 9 8 6 4 2

Stauffer, Stacey, 1973-
   Will Smith / by Stacey Stauffer.
   p.   cm. — (Black Americans of achievement)
Discography: p.
Filmography: p.
Includes bibliographical references and index.
ISBN 0-7910-4914-0
      0-7910-4915-9 (pbk.)
1. Smith, Will—Juvenile literature. 2. Motion picture actors and actresses—United States—Biography—Juvenile literature. 3. Afro-American motion picture actors and actresses—Biography—Juvenile literature. I.Title. II. Series.
PN2287.S612S72   1998
791.43'028'092—dc21   98-18551
[B]   CIP
                                                            AC

Frontis:
Will Smith—The Fresh Prince—in a lighthearted moment.

CONTENTS

—— ✿ ——

BLACK AMERICANS OF ACHIEVEMENT

HENRY AARON
baseball great

KAREEM ABDUL-JABBAR
basketball great

MUHAMMAD ALI
heavyweight champion

RICHARD ALLEN
*religious leader and
social activist*

MAYA ANGELOU
author

LOUIS ARMSTRONG
musician

ARTHUR ASHE
tennis great

JOSEPHINE BAKER
entertainer

JAMES BALDWIN
author

BENJAMIN BANNEKER
scientist and mathematician

AMIRI BARAKA
poet and playwright

COUNT BASIE
bandleader and composer

ROMARE BEARDEN
artist

JAMES BECKWOURTH
frontiersman

MARY MCLEOD BETHUNE
educator

GEORGE WASHINGTON
CARVER
botanist

CHARLES CHESNUTT
author

BILL COSBY
entertainer

PAUL CUFFE
merchant and abolitionist

MILES DAVIS
musician

FATHER DIVINE
religious leader

FREDERICK DOUGLASS
abolitionist editor

CHARLES DREW
physician

W. E. B. DU BOIS
scholar and activist

PAUL LAURENCE DUNBAR
poet

DUKE ELLINGTON
bandleader and composer

RALPH ELLISON
author

JULIUS ERVING
basketball great

LOUIS FARRAKHAN
political activist

ELLA FITZGERALD
singer

MARCUS GARVEY
black nationalist leader

JOSH GIBSON
baseball great

WHOOPI GOLDBERG
entertainer

ALEX HALEY
author

PRINCE HALL
social reformer

JIMI HENDRIX
musician

MATTHEW HENSON
explorer

BILLIE HOLIDAY
singer

LENA HORNE
entertainer

WHITNEY HOUSTON
singer and actress

LANGSTON HUGHES
poet

ZORA NEALE HURSTON
author

JESSE JACKSON
civil-rights leader and politician

MICHAEL JACKSON
entertainer

JACK JOHNSON
heavyweight champion

MAGIC JOHNSON
basketball great

SCOTT JOPLIN
composer

BARBARA JORDAN
politician

MICHAEL JORDAN
basketball great

CORETTA SCOTT KING
civil-rights leader

MARTIN LUTHER KING, JR.
civil-rights leader

LEWIS LATIMER
scientist

SPIKE LEE
filmmaker

CARL LEWIS
champion athlete

JOE LOUIS
heavyweight champion

RONALD MCNAIR
astronaut

MALCOLM X
militant black leader

BOB MARLEY
musician

THURGOOD MARSHALL
Supreme Court justice

TONI MORRISON
author

ELIJAH MUHAMMAD
religious leader

EDDIE MURPHY
entertainer

JESSE OWENS
champion athlete

SATCHEL PAIGE
baseball great

CHARLIE PARKER
musician

ROSA PARKS
civil-rights leader

COLIN POWELL
military leader

PAUL ROBESON
singer and actor

JACKIE ROBINSON
baseball great

DIANA ROSS
entertainer

WILL SMITH
actor

CLARENCE THOMAS
Supreme Court justice

SOJOURNER TRUTH
antislavery activist

HARRIET TUBMAN
antislavery activist

NAT TURNER
slave revolt leader

DENMARK VESEY
slave revolt leader

ALICE WALKER
author

MADAM C. J. WALKER
entrepreneur

BOOKER T. WASHINGTON
educator

DENZEL WASHINGTON
actor

OPRAH WINFREY
entertainer

TIGER WOODS
golf star

RICHARD WRIGHT
author

ON
ACHIEVEMENT

———— ❦ ————

Coretta Scott King

Before you begin this book, I hope you will ask yourself what the word *excellence* means to you. I think it's a question we should all ask, and keep asking as we grow older and change. Because the truest answer to it should never change. When you think of excellence, perhaps you think of success at work; or of becoming wealthy; or meeting the right person, getting married, and having a good family life.

Those goals are worth striving for, but there is a better way to look at excellence. As Martin Luther King Jr. said in one of his last sermons, "I want you to be first in love. I want you to be first in moral excellence. I want you to be first in generosity. If you want to be important, wonderful. If you want to be great, wonderful. But recognize that he who is greatest among you shall be your servant."

My husband knew that the true meaning of achievement is service. When I met him, in 1952, he was already ordained as a Baptist minister and was working toward a doctoral degree at Boston University. I was studying at the New England Conservatory and dreamed of accomplishments in music. We married a year later, and after I graduated the following year we moved to Montgomery, Alabama. We didn't know it then, but our notions of achievement were about to undergo a dramatic change.

You may have read or heard about what happened next. What began with the boycott of a local bus line grew into a national crusade, and by the time he was assassinated in 1968 my husband had fashioned a black movement powerful enough to shatter forever the practice of racial segregation. What you may not have read about is where he learned to resist injustice without compromising his religious beliefs.

He adopted a strategy of nonviolence from a man of a different race, who lived in a different country and even practiced a different religion. The man was Mahatma Gandhi, the great leader of India, who devoted his life to serving humanity in the spirit of love and nonviolence. It was in these principles that Martin discovered his method for social reform. More than anything else, those two principles were the key to his achievements.

These books are about African Americans who served society through the excellence of their achievements. They form part of the rich history of black men and women in America—a history of stunning accomplishments in every field of human endeavor, from literature and art to science, industry, education, diplomacy, athletics, jurisprudence, even polar exploration.

Not all of the people in this history had the same ideals, but I think you will find that all of them had something in common. Like Martin Luther King Jr., they all decided to become "drum majors" and serve humanity. In that principle—whether it was expressed in books, inventions, or song—they found a goal and a guide outside themselves that showed them a way to serve others instead of living only for themselves.

Reading the stories of these courageous men and women not only helps us discover the principles that we will use to guide our own lives; it also teaches us about our black heritage and about America itself. It is crucial for us to know the heroes and heroines of our history and to realize that the price we paid in our struggle for equality in America was dear. But we must also understand that we have gotten as far as we have partly because America's democratic system and ideals made it possible.

We are still struggling with racism and prejudice. But the great men and women in this series are a tribute to the spirit of the country in which they have flourished. And that makes their stories special and worth knowing.

1

INDEPENDENCE DAY

❧

IT TOOK WILL SMITH five years to become a successful rap musician and three more years to become a television star. But he went from being a highly regarded young entertainer to an international movie star in just a few days, when the blockbuster film *Independence Day* was released on the Fourth of July weekend in 1996.

Prior to the release of *Independence Day* (also known as *ID4*), Will was steadily working his way up the ladder of Hollywood success. After making a career as an award-winning rapper, half of the duo DJ Jazzy Jeff and the Fresh Prince, Will was introduced to a new audience as the star of the television sitcom *The Fresh Prince of Bel-Air*. He expanded his acting career in movies with an acclaimed performance in *Six Degrees of Separation* and good reviews for his acting in the action film *Bad Boys*. But by the end of July 1996 Will Smith was a household name, thanks to the incredible success of *Independence Day*.

The plot of the movie is simple, mirroring many science-fiction movies of the past. Visitors from outer space come to earth and attempt to destroy the planet. Will plays the role of Captain Steven Hiller, a fearless Marine fighter pilot who, when not battling the aliens and helping to save the world, cracks the audience up with his witty one-liners in the face of dangerous situations. The other stars of the film

Will Smith and Jeff Goldblum prepare to save the earth in the 1996 blockbuster film Independence Day.

include Jeff Goldblum, who plays David Levinson, the eccentric computer genius who first figures out the aliens' plans to destroy earth; Bill Pullman, portraying a former fighter pilot who is president of the United States; and Randy Quaid, whose character is an alcoholic crop duster who claims he was abducted by aliens years earlier and now wants to get revenge. In addition to the talented cast, the film has impressive special effects, including shots of the destruction of Moscow, Tokyo, London, Los Angeles, and such American symbols as the White House, the Empire State building, and the Statue of Liberty.

The film's producers were so excited about *Independence Day* that they operated a full-scale media blitz to spread the word. Before *Independence Day* was released, previews featuring its great special effects appeared on television, in movie theaters, and on posters. The hype surrounding *ID4* was so great that thousands of people camped out in front of movie theaters to get tickets to the premiere of the film on July 2, 1996. Some theaters showed the movie around the clock during the three-day holiday weekend. A huge theater in Washington, D.C.—with a two-story-high screen, an incredible sound system, and seating for 900 people—sold out all of its shows the first two days and had nearly full houses for the next several days.

Many of the movie critics who reviewed *Independence Day* seemed to enjoy it as much as the other viewers. "The grandest film of the summer. *ID4* is a sensation machine; you leave saying 'Wow!',", exclaimed *Time* magazine. *Rolling Stone* raved, "*ID4* delivers a full throttle blast. It gives you aliens to hiss at, humans to root for, and the kind of fireworks that get audiences cheering." *New York* magazine's simple statement revealed many viewers' feelings about the film: "This movie is undeniably fun." Another reviewer commented, "I don't know when I have enjoyed a movie as much as *Independence Day*. . . . [It]

achieves what so many films can't, a balance between action, humor and character."

Independence Day broke nearly every moneymaking record set by previous blockbuster films. It earned more money in a single day and in a weekend than any other movie ever had. It reached the $100 million mark faster than any other film, crossing that barrier in just seven days. (The 1993 blockbuster Jurassic Park had earned $100 million in nine days.) Independence Day continued to hold its sales momentum and break records by surpassing the $150 million mark in 12 days and the $200 million mark in 21 days. The movie wound up making more than $286

Captain Steven Hiller, the character Will plays in ID4, is a crack fighter pilot who is ordered to attack the enemy aliens threatening the planet. In this briefing scene, he is seated next to a fellow pilot played by Harry Connick Jr. Will's serious-but-humorous character contributed to the incredible success of the film.

(Continued on page 16)

Two high-ranking U.S. Air Force officers, Brigadier General Roger Ramey, commanding general of the Eighth Air Force, and Colonel Thomas Dubose, Eighth Air Force chief of staff, examine metallic fragments of an object that crashed near Roswell, New Mexico, in 1947. The military explanation was that a high-altitude weather balloon had crashed in the desert, but to this day many people believe that the incident actually involved a flying saucer and that the government had covered up proof of alien visitors.

IS THERE ANYBODY OUT THERE?

Why did *Independence Day*, a movie about an alien invasion, attract so many viewers? Perhaps it is because many people believe in extraterrestrials—visitors from other planets. In 1996 *Newsweek* reported that 48 percent of Americans believe in UFOs and 29 percent think humans have made contact with aliens.

There has always been an interest in the possibility of extraterrestrial life. In the late 19th and early 20th centuries, the writings of Jules Verne (*From the Earth to the Moon*) and H. G. Wells (*The War of the Worlds, The First Men in the Moon*) increased interest in space travel and alien civilizations. A 1938 radio adaptation of Wells's novel *The War of the Worlds* was mistaken for an actual alien attack and caused panic in New York and New Jersey. Orson Welles, who broadcast the story, neglected to make it clear that the report was fiction and not real news. Believing the earth was actually being taken over by aliens, listeners were frantic.

An incident that occurred nine years later, on June 14, 1947, further stirred belief in flying saucers and visitors from outer space. On that night, an object described as a "hexagonal flying saucer with strange markings" crashed onto a ranch in Roswell, New Mexico. Soldiers from a nearby army base removed the debris from the ranch. The official government report said that the flying object was, in fact, a modified weather/spy balloon used to test atmospheric conditions for signs of nuclear testing by the Soviet Union. However, rumors persisted that the object was a spacecraft. Two observers reported that they had seen a large, blue glowing object traveling through the sky at a high rate of speed the night before.

What actually happened on that June night still remains a mystery to the American people, but many believe that an alien spacecraft crashed at Roswell and that the government has covered up evidence to this effect while continuing to study the craft's remains at a secret air force base in Nevada. After the Roswell incident, more people began reporting Unidentified Flying Objects, or UFOs. Some of these reports have been discredited as hoaxes, but others have never been explained.

Historically, many science-fiction books and movies have successfully targeted the very same interest as *Independence Day*. Movies such as *E.T.* and *Close Encounters of the Third Kind* featured meetings with friendly aliens, while television shows such as *Star Trek* and *Battlestar Galactica* showed humans battling aliens in outer space. In the late 1990s, the television show *The X-Files*, featuring two FBI agents confronted by the possibility of alien contact with humans, became wildly popular, proving that speculation about the existence of extraterrestrials still fascinates many people.

Will Smith received a Blockbuster Entertainment Award for Favorite Male in a Science Fiction Film, along with rave reviews from critics and fans alike, for his role in Independence Day.

(Continued from page 13)

million, and with video sales, film industry observers speculated that it would be one of the highest-grossing films of all time.

Why was *Independence Day* such a blockbuster? Although some argued that it was simply because of the movie studio's superb marketing campaign, advertising isn't what makes a movie. In fact, sometimes publicity raises the public's expectations, and they are disappointed if the film doesn't measure up. With *Independence Day*, people expected a lot and got more than they hoped for. Certainly it helped to have experienced writers and producers, such as Dean Devlin and Roland Emmerich, who also cowrote the box-office hit *Stargate* in 1994, but even good direction doesn't mean a film will succeed. It is often the performances of the stars that can make or break a movie.

Will Smith's portrayal of the cigar-chomping Captain Hiller was an important part of *Independence Day*'s success. Audiences immediately liked the serious pilot who, although he is trying to save the earth, always comes up with hilarious comments and wisecracks, especially at some of the most crucial moments. One audience favorite was the scene in which he punches out an alien whose spacecraft crash-landed nearby, then cockily comments, "Welcome to Earth." "Audiences identify with him—I'd see it in their eyes at test screenings," said *ID4*'s director, Roland Emmerich.

Playing the part was a new experience for the young actor. "[Captain Hiller is] interesting because he's definitely serious, but he's also able to be funny," Will observed. "I've never experimented with that before. It's either been one or the other." Including an element of humor in a movie about the end of the world helped make *Independence Day* such a big sensation. That and the unbelievable special effects.

Just as if he had truly saved the world from invading aliens, Will Smith became a familiar face to many viewers after his performance in *Independence Day*. Even the critics who claimed that the film's plot was "unoriginal and predictable" praised Will for the level of humor and entertainment he added to the film. *Newsweek* captured his immediate rise to fame: "At 27, he's got one of the most impressively varied resumés in young Hollywood. . . . With *Independence Day*, he goes from big star to really, really big star." Shortly after the release of *Independence Day*, *Ebony* magazine called him a "rapper–turned television actor–turned movie star and bona fide celebrity." Although some people may not have recognized the name Will Smith before July 2, 1996, only those from another planet would not have recognized it thereafter. Viewers may have come to see *Independence Day* because of the storyline and the hype, but they left the theaters wanting to see more of Will Smith.

Will Smith, on filming *Independence Day*:

"In a scene with an alien, you're talking to air, or a sign that says 'Alien.' . . . [for cockpit scenes during the dogfights, the director] stood off-camera, saying, 'There's an explosion to your left! Now the plane dips to your right!' I heard all this and was thinking, 'Wait, I never knew this is what Han Solo had to go through.'"

2

BORN LAUGHING

✿

WILL SMITH WAS BORN in Children's Hospital, Philadelphia, on September 25, 1968—a tumultuous year in the United States. In the months before he was born, a wave of violence and protests inundated a nation that was mourning the deaths of two great leaders, Martin Luther King Jr. and Robert F. Kennedy.

Martin Luther King Jr. was a civil rights leader who had devoted his life to fighting for the rights of African Americans and ending racial discrimination. He advocated nonviolent methods to bring about change, and under his leadership the civil rights movement of the 1950s and '60s made great strides. His finest moment may have been his organization of a massive civil rights march in Washington, D.C., on August 28, 1963. Standing in the shadow of the Lincoln Memorial, King delivered his stirring "I Have a Dream" speech, looking toward a day when all races would be united and a person's character would not be judged by the color of his or her skin. Unfortunately, he would not live to see that day; King was gunned down on April 4, 1968, in Memphis, Tennessee, where he had been organizing a protest march. The violent death of this peaceful man sparked rioting in black neighborhoods throughout the country.

King was not the only important political figure assassinated in 1968. Just two months later, presiden-

Will Smith as a senior at Overbrook High School in Philadelphia, where he grew up.

In this home in the Wynnefield neighborhood of Philadelphia, the Smith children—Pam, Willard Jr., Ellen, and Harry—were raised by their parents, Willard and Caroline Smith.

tial candidate Robert F. Kennedy was also shot and killed. The younger brother of former president John F. Kennedy, who had been assassinated in 1963, Robert Kennedy was considered the political hope of a new generation. He was supported by people from all walks of life—young people, blue-collar workers, professionals, and minorities—and he had just won California's Democratic primary (each political party holds a primary election to decide who its candidate for president will be in the general election in November) when he was shot in his hotel on the way to his victory celebration.

However, in 1968 there were some signs that racial barriers were dropping for American blacks. An African-American tennis player named Arthur Ashe became the first black man to win a major tennis title with his victory in the U.S. National Amateur singles competition. He also won the U.S. Open later in the year and became the first black to play on the U.S. Davis Cup team. On August 21, 1968, James Anderson Jr. became the first African-American Marine to be awarded the Medal of Honor for his service in Vietnam. This was the world into which Caroline and Willard Smith Sr., an African-American couple living in Philadelphia, brought their second child. They named the little boy Willard Smith Jr.

Willard Smith Sr. was the owner of a company that designed and repaired supermarket refrigeration units. Will's mother, Caroline, worked as an administrator for the local board of education. They already had a daughter, Pamela, who was five years older than Will. Two years after he was born, the Smiths added two more children to the family with the birth of twins, Harry and Ellen.

Will and his family lived in a brick row house in a middle-class neighborhood called Wynnefield. The original homes in this neighborhood had been built in the late 19th and early 20th century. Between 1910 and 1940, during West Philadelphia's rapid urbanization, row homes designed for middle-class families were built in Wynnefield. Over the years, the neighborhood became predominantly black. When Will was growing up, he often heard stories about notable former Wynnefield residents, such as astronaut Guion Bluford and basketball star Wilt Chamberlain.

As a young child Will enjoyed listening to his parents read Dr. Seuss books because of their jovial rhymes. In fact, years later Will said his love for rap rhymes stemmed from the books he read in childhood. "If you listen to them a certain way, books like *Green Eggs and Ham* and *Hop on Pop* sound a lot like hip-hop," he once told a reporter.

When he was old enough, Will attended Our Lady of Lourdes, a nearby parochial elementary school, where he excelled in English, math, and science and was known as the class clown. He also developed a particular interest in dinosaurs (his favorite was the stegosaurus), and learned not just the names but the eras in which different dinosaurs lived. But his parents had always taught their children that there was a lot to be learned outside of the classroom. Seven-year-old Will found this to be true when his family drove across the United States to see some of the country's major landmarks: Yellowstone National Park, Mount Rushmore, the Alamo, and the Grand Canyon. "You see something beautiful, bigger than you, and it mellows you, changes your attitude for life," Will reflected years later.

Will Smith, on his parents:

"There are individual personality traits of celebrities and sports stars I admire, but the only people I continue to idolize are my parents. They taught me clearly the difference between right and wrong, and that when you make a mistake you must be honest with yourself about it."

Young Will Smith seemed to find fun in just about every aspect of growing up—at home, with his friends, or at school. Even as a youngster he had the ability to make people laugh, and he found that he had a gift for entertaining. In the biography *Will Power!*, Smith is quoted as saying, "It's always been fun for me to tell a story and make people laugh. I've always been a show-off. I only got uncomfortable when people *weren't* looking at me. . . . I was blessed with a really, really funny family. Dinnertime was like a nightly laugh riot."

Will used his humor, and not his looks, to develop new friends at school and in the neighborhood. "When I was little, everybody always told me I looked

like Alfred E. Newman, the weird guy on the cover of *Mad* magazine," he later told an interviewer. "I always had that square-looking fade hairdo, and I liked it, even though it made my ears stick out. One guy once told me I looked like a car with the doors open."

Will's parents instilled in their children a love of music, and all were encouraged to sing and play instruments. Will learned how to play the piano because it was his mother's favorite instrument, but recalls that he played a little bit of everything because instruments were strewn throughout the Smith home. This affinity for music, fostered from an early age, eventually led Will to a career as a rapper, and beyond. In the first episode of his television series *The Fresh Prince of Bel Air*, Will sat down at a piano and spontaneously played a sonata by Beethoven, *Für*

Will was known as the class clown when he attended Our Lady of Lourdes, a nearby parochial school.

Growing up, Will spent a lot of time playing basketball on the playgrounds near his home. This court was just a block away from the Smith household.

Elise, because it was something that he remembered from his childhood.

Will was supported in his early musical and entertainment endeavors by his family, especially his grandmother, Helen Bright. She was very active in the local Baptist Church and encouraged her grandchildren to attend services weekly. Will owes his first onstage performance to his grandmother, who placed him in one of the church holiday plays. However, although he enjoyed being in the spotlight, Will's first childhood dream was not to become a popular musician or entertainer. Instead, he wanted to become an astronaut.

Some of Will Smith's favorite television programs, such as *Laverne and Shirley, Happy Days,* and *Three's Company,* may have led to his interest in a career entertaining others. His love for making people laugh was strengthened by his favorite star, a highly successful African-American comedian named Eddie Murphy. He watched Murphy in each of his hilarious routines on *Saturday Night Live* and later in movies like *Beverly Hills Cop* and *48 Hours*, and dreamed that one day he would be compared to this extraordinarily successful star.

Although Eddie Murphy was one of his idols growing up, Will Smith's greatest role models were his parents. Will's parents showered their family with love and attention—and discipline when it was necessary. Because of Will's antics—"Will did the gross things kids do, like put straws up his nose," sister Ellen recalled years later—and his position as the oldest boy, he often was punished before his younger brother, Harry, or his sisters. In a 1996 *People* magazine article, Harry recalled that after they were punished Will would "go around a corner and make faces so we'd laugh—and we'd get punished worse."

Will's father was the disciplinarian of the family. Will may have been the class clown, but he knew when to stop fooling around. Thanks to the discipline instilled by Willard Smith Sr., his son never fell prey to peer pressure like some of the other youths in his neighborhood. "Even with peer pressure, there wasn't a friend I had who could pressure me to do something I knew would get me into trouble with my father," Will is quoted as saying in *Will Power!* "My father had so much control over me when I was growing up—I didn't have too much of an opportunity to do things the wrong way. My father was always in my business. He always knew everything I was doing! He was always there to make sure I knew what the right way was. He was the man with all the answers, the disciplinarian. He did his shaping up by taking little chunks out of your behind!"

Will's father also taught by example: once, when Will was a teenager, father and son drove through a bad section of Philadelphia, where drug addicts slept on street corners and in the doorways of abandoned, run-down houses. "He pointed to the bums sleeping in the doorways and said, 'This is what people look like when they do drugs.'" One look was enough to convince Will to stay away from drugs.

Will's parents also taught their children the importance of believing in themselves. One summer Will Sr. insisted that his sons rebuild a brick wall that was deteriorating. Will and Harry spent several months tearing down the old wall and building a new one. When they were finished, their father said, "Now don't ever tell me that you can't do something"—advice Will Smith has never forgotten. "I look back on a lot of times in my life when I think I won't be able to do something," he is quoted in *Will Power!* "Then I think about that wall, and tell myself, 'one brick at a time.'"

In addition to these lessons, Will's parents taught their children to be honest. Caroline and Willard tried to make the best possible choices for their family and hoped that their children would always make the right decisions, but they also taught Will and his siblings to be honest if they made a mistake.

Will's parents were honest with their children even when it came to the most challenging and difficult trial that their family had to face. When Willard and Caroline Smith decided to divorce, 13-year-old Will had to learn that his family would still be held together by love even though his parents would no longer live together. "We never felt our parents didn't love us," he later told an interviewer. "No matter how difficult things got, or how angry someone might have gotten, no matter what happened in our lives, we always felt like we had somewhere to go.

"You can't spring off into the world from a flimsy base, you've got to have a solid base to jump from," Will continued. "My parents, together or apart, provided that base."

Will continued to live with his mother after the divorce, but he saw his father as often as possible. The teenager often worked at his father's shop after school. He also found himself becoming involved in a new craze that was becoming popular in the early 1980s: rap music.

3

OVERNIGHT SUCCESS

❦

In 1980, a musical group called the Sugar Hill Gang released *Rapper's Delight*. This record proved to be the beginning of a new music genre, rap, that gained national attention and would grow in popularity over the next decade. For 12-year-old Will Smith, it sparked an interest in rap, or "hip-hop," which years later would propel him into the music industry.

Rap music quickly became popular not only because of its unique sounds and fast-paced beat but also because rappers included the visual effect of break dancing and other interesting moves when performing. Rap music's audience continued to increase and it hit a peak with huge hits by rap/rock groups such as the Beastie Boys and Run-D.M.C. in 1986. (In an interview at the end of 1997, Will admitted that Run-D.M.C. was his favorite group of all time.)

For Will Smith and many other young men, especially African Americans, rap was more than music. It was an expression of life. When Will wasn't at school, working, sleeping, or eating, he was rapping. He had started out as a disk jockey (or DJ) playing records at neighborhood parties, but soon his instinctive desire to perform broke out. By the time he was 13, Will Smith had a reputation as one of the best new rappers in Philadelphia.

When he was 15, Will entered Overbrook High School in Philadelphia, where he continued with his

DJ Jazzy Jeff (Jeff Townes) and the Fresh Prince (Will Smith) show off their American Music Award for Best Album. The duo's first single, "Girls Ain't Nothing but Trouble," was a surprise hit that soon made them one of the most popular rap acts.

role as class clown and also received the nickname "Prince," as in Prince Charming, because he was always able to charm his way out of trouble. Will wasn't an outstanding student in school; in a *People* article, he recalled a teacher complaining to his mother that Will "was testing at a college level but just barely passing." Under pressure from mom, he improved his grades.

"Study was not his primary concern, but he was a solid student," commented Ronald Matthews, Will's 11th grade American History teacher at Overbrook. "He was a thorn for me. Not actually in a negative sense. Will could be disruptive in a comical sense." Matthews noted that singling out talkative kids in class usually embarrassed them into being quiet and paying attention. However, Smith always withstood the embarrassment and then dished out his own in retaliation. "He could make a class laugh," Matthews admitted.

Will was a member of the chess club at Overbrook High. Chess was a game that he started learning at an early age—his father taught him how to play when Will was eight. When he was 14, Will beat his father for the first time. "I saw the checkmate coming, and I was petrified," he later admitted. But Will feels it was important that he had to earn the victory. "It built my self-esteem."

At Overbrook, Will was the featured DJ at his junior and senior prom. He was also part of Overbrook High School's "Motivation Program," a college-prep program that exposed students to cultural events such as plays. There were about 2,500 students at the high school, and fewer than 10 percent were admitted to the Motivation Program, whose members were a select group chosen by the faculty. The program was geared toward college-bound students, and Will's teachers told him that he needed to have an alternative to a music career, in case he did not succeed as a rap musician.

With the support of his parents and teachers, Will graduated from Overbrook in 1986. His mother was pleased when he was accepted by the Massachusetts Institute of Technology (MIT), one of the best schools in the country. He was also accepted by the Milwaukee School of Engineering. However, Will had other plans—his career as a rapper.

While in high school Will had been performing with a friend, Clate Holmes, who called himself Ready Rock-C. Will wrote some material, and the two of them offered it to a well-known rap producer named Dana Goodman. Although Goodman liked Will's work, there was not enough material to fill an entire album, and he suggested that they keep working. Will was preparing new material when he met another local rap star, Jeff Townes.

At Overbrook High School, Will (fourth row, fifth from left) was a member of the Motivation Program, a select group of students that participated in extracurricular educational activities. Most of the students in this group expected to go to college; however, although Will had been accepted at MIT and at the Milwaukee School of Engineering, he instead decided to put higher education on hold and focus on a career in music.

Jeff, who called himself DJ Jazzy Jeff, was four years older than Will Smith. The 20-year-old had been one of the top hip-hop DJs for several years. Both Jeff and Will had grown up in Philadelphia. They had heard about each other but had never met until 1985 when Jeff was the disk jockey at a party in Will's neighborhood. Jeff later remembered:

> I was the best DJ in Philadelphia and I had heard of Will, but I already had someone that I worked with. But when I played that party on Will's block, naturally he was there. He asked if he could rap for a while and I said yes. He started rapping and I started cutting, and it was like natural chemistry. He flowed with what I did and I flowed exactly with what he did and we knew it. We just clicked the whole night long. The chemistry between us was so good.

They began working together from that night on, performing at parties, clubs, and church functions. They also became good friends. Will and Jeff had the same sense of humor, and at parties where they played, people were entertained as much by their jokes as by their music. "I bought this canned fart spray and sprayed it at a party," Jeff remembered. "We just cracked up. When I found Will was down with the same humor, that was when we really clicked." The duo's popularity continued to grow as their talents became more recognized in their local neighborhoods.

After school and on weekends, Will and Jeff met in Jeff's basement, which had been transformed into a small recording studio. First they would discuss ideas and their own experiences, which were the foundation of their songs, and then they would begin working on the songs. Jeff wrote the music as Will composed the lyrics.

When it came time to name their group, Will decided that he needed a nickname. Jeff was going to keep his well-known nickname, DJ Jazzy Jeff, so Will decided to modify his high-school nickname,

"Prince." He added the adjective "fresh," meaning "the best" or "cool," and so the rap duo DJ Jazzy Jeff and the Fresh Prince was born.

Once they believed they had plenty of good material, Will, then an Overbrook senior, and Jeff handed over their demo tapes to the same producer Will had approached a few years earlier, Dana Goodman. This time, Goodman signed the pair to an independent rap record label, Word Up. Soon their first single, "Girls Ain't Nothing but Trouble," was released.

The song, about the uncertainty of teenage romance, quickly became popular among young people because most of them could relate to it. In a short time, "Girls Ain't Nothing but Trouble" was a major hit, selling over 100,000 copies in the U.S. and becoming a Top 20 hit in England. Because of the success of the single, another record label, Jive Records, bought the rights to the single and brought Smith and Townes into the studio to record an album. *Rock The House*, their debut recording, was an immediate success, selling 600,000 copies. Within a few months, before Will had even graduated from high school, the duo had shot from obscurity to a top position in the rap genre. By the next year, Will and Jeff were asked to join the international Def Jam tour, which featured rappers like LL Cool J and Public Enemy.

Will Smith, on his beginnings in show business:

"It kind of developed for me naturally. I started out rapping as a hobby and everything developed from that hobby. I never made a conscious decision that I wanted to be in show business. I was there, I was prepared, and it presented itself."

However, there was a negative side to all of this publicity. Some critics viewed "Girls Ain't Nothing but Trouble" as a sexist song. Will, who respected his mother, sisters, and grandmother, took offense at this criticism. "That's a ridiculous, idiotic opinion," he slammed back at the song's detractors. "The rap is a personal story, told with a sense of humor, rather than a statement of general attitude." Will and Jeff would, however, confront this judgement in a

The cover of Will's Overbrook High yearbook in his senior year, 1986 (right). The candid photo of Will (above) that was part of a collage at the beginning of the book was captioned, "How does this thing work, anyway?"

humorous way by releasing a companion song, entitled "Guys Ain't Nothing but Trouble."

Because of the success of *Rock The House*, Will decided not to go to college. Instead he would focus on his career. According to *Will Power!*, although Will's parents were not happy with this decision, his father allowed Will to follow his dream, telling him, "Okay. Take a year [to continue with rap]. If it works, God bless you. If it doesn't, you'll go to college."

Will's decision proved to be a sound one: DJ Jazzy Jeff and the Fresh Prince released their second album in 1988. Entitled *He's the DJ, I'm the Rapper*, it included the duo's biggest hit, "Parents Just Don't Understand." It is a song that makes listeners both laugh and nod their heads in agreement. All teenagers understand the horrors of going shopping with their mothers, and Will told the story with the skill of a professional comedian. *He's the DJ, I'm the Rapper* went platinum, meaning it sold over one million copies.

The next year, 1989, was a great year for the duo. In addition to releasing another successful album, *And in This Corner*, which also went platinum, in January DJ Jazzy Jeff and the Fresh Prince won the Best Rap Album and Best Rap Artist categories at the annual American Music Awards. A month later, the two became the first performers to win a Grammy Award in the newly added rap category when "Parents Just Don't Understand" was named Best Rap Single.

A minor scandal occurred when Will and Jeff declined to attend the Grammy Award ceremony to accept their award. The rap category was not viewed by the event organizers as very important, so the award would be presented as a nontelevised event along with some technical awards. Will and Jeff decided to make a statement by not showing up to receive the award because they believed the committee was wrong. After that incident, the rap category became a

NINETEEN NINETEEN NINETEEN NINETEEN EIGHTY SIX EIGHTY SIX EIGHTY SIX EIGHTY SIX

OVERBROOK HIGH SCHOOL *Record*

59th E. Lancaster Avenue
Philadelphia, Pennsylvania

part of the televised portion of the Grammys.

To Will Smith and Jeff Townes, the Grammy committee's snub was less upsetting than criticism the duo received from the hardcore rap community, which accused them of being "too soft." While most rap groups were singing about drug dealers, killers, street life, and other negative aspects of their world, DJ Jazzy Jeff and the Fresh Prince wrote songs about their everyday life. Some rappers considered them to be fakes and accused them of ignoring the issues that African Americans had to deal with so that their music would appeal to the mainstream culture. Rappers such as Big Daddy Kane accused DJ Jazzy Jeff and the Fresh Prince of creating music intentionally for white people who didn't understand the foundation of rap. Will and Jeff were crushed by this accusation. The songs they wrote were based on their own experiences—they couldn't rap about violence or drugs or killings because they hadn't experienced those things. If they tried, they felt, they *would* be fakes. Will and Jeff responded to Kane's criticism in an interview with *USA Today*:

> I don't think anyone can dictate what's black and what's not black. Big Daddy Kane is ignorant and doesn't realize what black really means. He thinks being articulate is being white. We're trying to show the world, and black kids, that you can dress nicely and speak well and still be considered black. Our music is black music. Our families are black, we came from black backgrounds. . . .
>
> We do rap from a different point of view. We make it fun. We make it universal. My point of view isn't limited. It's very broad. It's more than the black experience.

Will and Jeff were also criticized for not using profanity in their rap, but Will responded, "I would never do anything that my mother couldn't turn on her radio and listen to. . . . I would never do anything to offend my family."

The point of Will and Jeff's music was simple: to have fun. They were having fun making the music, and wanted people to have fun while listening. Because of Will's storytelling skills, their best songs were the ones that told a story: "Girls Ain't Nothing But Trouble," "Parents Just Don't Understand," and "I Think I Can Beat Mike Tyson." Jeff's mixing, scratching, and sound effects provided a solid backbone for the duo, and Jeff also proved his versatility as one of the few DJs that could also rap. He was featured on several tracks, such as "Men of Your Dreams."

The music of DJ Jazzy Jeff and the Fresh Prince certainly appealed to a wide audience. This was evident from their increasing number of fans who were of different races from all over the world. Their success made Will Smith a millionaire before his 18th birthday. However, Jeff and Will were riding a wave of success that would soon crash down on top of them.

4

FROM BROKE TO BEL-AIR

❧

IMAGINE GOING TO BED with a million dollars in the bank and waking up the next day to find it gone. That's how Will Smith felt in 1990 when he learned that he was broke—he owed the Internal Revenue Service (IRS) millions of dollars in income taxes, and no money had been set aside to pay them.

With success and fame came money—a lot of money. Thanks to their almost-immediate success, Will and Jeff received a steady flow of large amounts of cash. In fact, by his 18th birthday, Will was a millionaire. And music was not the only way that Will and Jeff were making money. They started an information line for fans of DJ Jazzy Jeff and the Fresh Prince to call and hear a message from the duo. Within the first six months, two million people called the 900 number, at $2.45 per call.

But Will and Jeff spent the money as fast as it came in. When they went on tour they hired several of their friends from Philadelphia to be dancers, bodyguards, and crew, and they took the whole entourage around the world to promote their music. They ate at expensive restaurants, rode around in limousines, and hung out with Hollywood stars. To record their third album, they took their entire sound crew, as well as many friends, to the Bahamas. This wasn't the only vacation Will took—he traveled spontaneously and often took friends along.

After his success as a rap artist, Will proved his versatility by starring in a successful television sitcom, The Fresh Prince of Bel-Air.

Besides traveling, Will spent an enormous amount of money on jewelry, cars, and clothes. He owned a number of automobiles, including a Corvette and a Camaro. Will wore gold and diamond jewelry and purchased a mansion in Merion, a suburb of Philadelphia, where he and his brother Harry lived when they weren't traveling. Will gambled in Las Vegas and Atlantic City and placed large bets in games with friends.

Will knew that he wasn't handling the money well, but he couldn't stop. "One year I spent $800,000," he was quoted as saying in *Will Power!* "I went through it so fast, it made my head spin. Being able to buy anything you want makes you a little crazy." He later told *People* magazine, "Money disappears a lot faster than it comes in, no matter how much you make."

After ten months of careless spending, reality smacked Will in the face when he learned that he owed the government millions of dollars because he had not put aside any of his earnings to cover his income taxes. "There's nothing more sobering than having six cars and a mansion one day, and you can't even buy gas for the cars the next," he later recalled.

With his money gone, Will realized he had strayed from the values he had been taught as a child. He vowed to remain the good-natured, sensible person that his parents had raised, despite any future success.

Will also had learned that money can't buy happiness or respect. Even as a millionaire he dealt with the problems of racism—whether it was a Philadelphia policeman who stopped him because he looked "suspicious" while he was cruising in a nice sports car, or a store attendant who watched his every move.

Once he committed himself to fiscal restraint, Will's money problems did not last long. Although no other album was able to match the success of *He's the DJ, I'm the Rapper*, which went triple platinum, by 1993 DJ Jazzy Jeff and the Fresh Prince had released

Although Will was making a lot of money because of the success of his records, he was spending it even faster. "Being able to buy anything you want makes you a little crazy," he later admitted.

two more successful albums, *Homebase* and *Code Red*. "Summertime," a single from *Homebase*, received a Grammy Award in 1991. Many people think "Summertime" is the group's best song, and Will himself admits it is one of his favorites: "I think it's one of the best things we've done." DJ Jazzy Jeff and the Fresh Prince won the NAACP Image Award in 1992 for Outstanding Rap Artist.

Although his music career was very successful, Will Smith wasn't satisfied. He wanted to develop other skills as a safety net in case his fortunes declined as a rapper. He had seen many other rap musicians' careers disappear after just a few hits, and

Quincy Jones, shown here receiving the NAACP's Entertainer of the Year award in 1996, was instrumental in creating The Fresh Prince of Bel-Air *for NBC.*

although he didn't believe this would happen to him, he had learned from his past experiences to be prepared for whatever life would hand him.

He had given some thought to the possibility of acting as a second career. And why not? After all, Will had been the class clown in school, he had played some parts in plays at church, and whether at a neighborhood party or on stage before thousands of fans, he had been recognized for his natural ability to perform.

In 1989 Will was on the set of *The Arsenio Hall Show* when he received his "break" into the acting world. Benny Medina, a Warner Music executive, was also on the set for a special tribute to music producer Quincy Jones. Medina had an idea for a television sitcom and discussed it with Will, who loved the idea and mentioned his desire to try acting.

Medina's sitcom idea was based loosely on his own life story. Orphaned at an early age and living in a poor neighborhood, he experienced a considerable amount of violence. He grew up in foster homes, and one in particular made an everlasting impact on Medina. He was placed with a well-off family in Beverly Hills. Medina found the lifestyle vastly different, yet he received love and affection from this new foster family that was not available on the streets. He became so close to his foster parents, the Elliots, that they eventually adopted Medina. Medina's adoptive father, Jack Elliot, was well known to the stars of Hollywood and other members of high society. This relationship offered many opportunities to Medina, who was creative, energetic, and ambitious.

Medina thought that this unusual story would be the ideal setting for a humorous TV show. Medina was also familiar with Will's song "Parents Just Don't Understand." As he spoke to Will he realized that the song not only addressed the many issues children and parents deal with on a daily basis but also was spiced with the type of humor Medina believed the show needed to be lighthearted and entertaining. As Medina spoke with Will that evening, he mentally placed Will in the lead role he envisioned for his show.

Without waiting any longer, Medina pitched the idea to Quincy Jones, who was known not only as a record producer but also as the creator of successful television shows and movies. Jones was enthusiastic and suggested pitching the idea to executives at one of the major television networks. He believed it would be best to approach NBC because of its family-oriented sitcoms that aired during prime time. His instincts were on track: NBC's eight o'clock sitcom, *ALF*, was beginning to fall in the ratings, and the

Will Smith, on keeping a level head:

"I was in the music business first, and it's really cutthroat and hard. So I had my ups and downs. Had money, then was broke. I kinda got my footing together before I got into television and the film world. Because this type of attention can make you crazy."

network was hungry for a new idea.

Jones invited the NBC executives over to his house to see Will Smith audition for the lead role in their new sitcom. Will was nervous; he knew that this was his chance to become an actor. However, when he performed for the NBC executives his natural ability to entertain and make people laugh was obvious. "Will read the script, put some of his personal nuances in it, and right after that everybody was shaking hands, hugging, and kissing," Benny Medina recalled in a *People* interview a year later. And NBC's entertainment president, Warren Littlefield, later said, "There were no beads of sweat. Will read from a script and nailed it. I sat there thinking, 'Whoa! Just bottle this guy!'" And with that Will Smith was on his way to television stardom on the sitcom *The Fresh Prince of Bel-Air*.

Although the idea for *The Fresh Prince of Bel-Air* was based on the life of Benny Medina, it mirrored Will's life as well. Although he was never homeless or poverty-stricken, Will had gone from being a part of an average, middle-class family to living the life of a millionaire. While his story wasn't the rags-to-riches story of Medina's, it was one that many people could enjoy. Even if they had not experienced his huge success, they were able to relate to Will's childhood and family, just as they could relate to the stories in his rap music.

The show's producers, Medina and Jones, decided to make the lead character more similar to Will while keeping the storyline that Medina had intended. They decided his character would move from Philadelphia to Beverly Hills. He would be a smart kid who wasn't applying himself in school and was getting into some trouble in the East, so he was sent to his uncle and aunt's home in a posh California town in an attempt to help him become mature. From this new family, Will, the Fresh Prince, was supposed to learn respect and discipline. As both

The Fresh Prince of Bel-Air *was similar in some ways to another NBC sitcom, The* Cosby Show, *which was a huge hit during the 1980s. Both shows portrayed happy, well-to-do black families dealing with the problems and issues that real families are faced with every day.*

Medina and Will had found in real life, *The Fresh Prince of Bel-Air* showed that the youth from Philadelphia had a lot to learn as he was thrown into a new society and different world, while the wealthy family that took him in discovered that they too could learn from their street-smart cousin.

Whether it was because people could identify with Will's character, because they loved his humor, or because they simply fell in love with his charm, *The Fresh Prince of Bel-Air* was a huge success. It was soon compared to a 1980s NBC hit, also about a black family: *The Cosby Show.* Although the shows' story lines were completely different, *The Cosby Show* and *The Fresh Prince of Bel-Air* had some similarities. Both shows were successful in large part due to the characters they portrayed, well-to-do African-American families. Both dealt with issues that all families could relate to, such as dating, drug and alcohol use, and discipline. The serious issues of day-to-day family life were peppered with an abundance of humor.

The characters in both shows also displayed love and affection for their family members. They showed that it was possible for families to be happy together and to love and support one another. As Will pointed out in a 1990 *People Weekly* interview, "What I am happiest about is that I can be a role model and give people something to think about. . . . It's important to have a black show that's positive. Television has been controlled by white America, and they've had a tendency to put their own on."

There were some distinct contrasts between the two shows because they portrayed different socioeconomic classes. *The Cosby Show* was about an upper-middle-class family that followed the tradition of happy television families such as the Cleavers in *Leave it to Beaver*, yet still brought the realities and uncertainties of life to the screen. *The Fresh Prince of Bel-Air* revealed the clash of two worlds—the middle class and the very rich. Also, the cultural differences of the East (Philadelphia) and West (Beverly Hills) Coasts fascinated viewers.

Just as popular comedian Bill Cosby had played the largest part in the success of *The Cosby Show*, Will Smith made *The Fresh Prince of Bel-Air* a hit. Both actors had the natural ability to make people feel at ease, smile, and laugh uncontrollably, and both did so in a tasteful and entertaining way. Both were able to inject impromptu humor into the script; this added not only to the comedy but also to the realism of the shows and the characters. Both actors also played characters based on themselves, which allowed viewers to get a sense of what Will Smith and Bill Cosby are like offscreen. Will even sang the theme song for the new show.

While both shows attracted audiences of all ages because they included characters of varying ages, the target age group of each show depended primarily on its star. Although families watched these shows together, adults were the main audience for *The Cosby Show*, while *The Fresh Prince of Bel-Air* attracted a younger audience that became interested in the fun-loving Will Smith.

5

THE FRESH PRINCE
OF BEL-AIR

────── ❧ ──────

THE PILOT EPISODE of *The Fresh Prince of Bel-Air* aired on September 10, 1990. In that first episode, Will moves from Philadelphia and meets the relatives with whom he will stay in Bel-Air, the Banks family.

The cast of *The Fresh Prince of Bel-Air* was a seasoned one whose members all had more acting experience than Will. Veteran actor James Avery, who had appeared on television shows, in films such as *Fletch*, and in made-for-TV movies, played Will's wealthy uncle, Philip Banks. Janet Hubert-Whitten, another experienced actor, played Will's aunt, Vivian Banks.

Besides Will, the most well-known cast member of *The Fresh Prince of Bel-Air* was Alfonso Ribeiro, who played Will's stuffy cousin, Carlton Banks. Ribeiro was best known for his role as Ricky Schroeder's best friend on the endearing television show *Silver Spoons*, which ran from 1984–1987, as well as for his parts in made-for-TV movies. Karyn Parsons, who played Will's ditzy cousin Hilary Banks, had appeared in films before doing the sitcom. Joseph Marcell, the sarcastic butler Geoffrey, had had both film and television roles, and even Tatyana Ali, who was much younger than Will and played his younger cousin, had much more acting experience. The daughter of renowned boxer

In the final season of The Fresh Prince of Bel-Air, *the cast included (front, left to right) Tatyana M. Ali (Ashley Banks), Will Smith, Alfonso Ribeiro (Carlton Banks), (back) Karyn Parsons (Hilary Banks), James Avery (Judge Philip Banks), Daphne Maxwell Reid (Vivian Banks), and Joseph Marcell (Geoffrey the butler). Reid had replaced Janet Hubert-Whitten, the original Aunt Vivian, after three seasons.*

49

Ashley, Carlton, Hilary, and Will converse in a popular meeting place: the Banks's kitchen. When the first episodes of The Fresh Prince aired in 1990, the other members of the cast all had much more acting experience than Will, even though he was billed as the star.

Muhammad Ali, Tatyana had appeared in commercials and in the 1987 movie *Crocodile Dundee II*.

It took some time for the cast to feel comfortable working together. There was certainly some tension on the set because the actors and actresses playing the supporting roles were more experienced than the lead character. Will understood their feelings and knew that he was in an unfavorable position because he had no one to be a mentor. There was enormous pressure placed on him to perform, yet he had no one to teach him the ins and outs of acting. Although he was comfortable when he was on stage rapping, it was impossible for Will to always contain his nervousness on-camera. He looked to producer Quincy Jones and his costars for help with his acting.

"I was trying so hard," Will said later. "I would

memorize the entire script, then I'd be mouthing everybody's lines right back at them—while they were talking. . . . My performances were horrible. . . . I was afraid of missing my lines." In *Will Power!*, costar Tatyana Ali said, "I couldn't believe what a bad actor he was. I'd do a scene with him and he would mouth my words while I was doing my lines. . . . If you look at the old shows, you can see it."

Will practiced daily, watched tapes of himself to see how to improve, and gradually became a much better actor. But from the first episode *The Fresh Prince of Bel-Air* received great ratings, and praise was poured on Will. Many fans of his music watched his transition from the concert stage to the television screen. And the character that Will portrayed on the show each week was so unique, clever, and crazy that the viewers never knew what to expect. He kept the audience on its toes with his witty one-liners, bizarre clothing, and mischievous grin. One thing that they could always expect was to get a few good laughs during the half-hour sitcom. Audiences warmed to Will immediately. Whatever it was about this young man that intrigued the prime-time viewers and made them smile would continue to make people of all ages adore Will and his work. People immediately began calling him "the next Eddie Murphy." This kind of pressure was almost more than Will could bear, and he tried to downplay the comparisons while praising his costars for their assistance. "Give me four or five years, and let me practice," he told *People* in 1990. "I am nowhere near Eddie Murphy."

In time, the cast members bonded and became close friends. One circumstance that helped the show's stars eventually became closer was Will's decision to make the shows more realistic. Although humor made the show highly entertaining, Will wanted more. He wanted *The Fresh Prince of Bel-Air* to be a show that was heartwarming but enlightening, dealing with tough issues, such as racism. He

Stuffy butler Geoffrey's acid-tongued comments and occasionally crazy antics (in this episode he threw a wild party when the Banks family visited Will's mother in Philadelphia) were among the reasons people enjoyed tuning in to The Fresh Prince *every week.*

wanted the Banks family to face the problems that viewers also faced; this would help people connect with the Bankses.

As he had been all his life, Will was a practical joker on the set of *The Fresh Prince of Bel-Air*. One time he wrapped a toilet seat in clear plastic; another time he talked a policeman into harassing one of his friends about some unpaid parking tickets. Although his victims may not have appreciated being the butt of Will's humor, the jokes always lightened the mood on the set.

Problems still cropped up on the show at times, however. Janet Hubert-Whitten became increasingly unhappy, and she left the show after the third season. Although her reasons for dissatisfaction were never truly known, there were rumors that Will had been responsible. He denied involvement. "[She] was an incredible actress. She brought so much spirit and fun and warmth to *The Fresh Prince of Bel-Air*. . . . I think the show suffered for the loss of Janet Hubert-Whitten," he said. Replaced by Daphne Reid in 1993, she was the only major character to leave the show. The next year, *The Fresh Prince of Bel-Air* welcomed a new member of the Banks family, Philip and Vivian's daughter Nicky.

One of Will's favorite episodes of *The Fresh Prince of Bel-Air* was the Christmas episode of 1992. In this show, the Banks family comes to realize that Christmas isn't about gifts and beautiful decorations, but about love and family. The show opens by focusing on an array of extravagant holiday decorations and highlighting the family's abundant wealth. But soon the joy is stripped away as the family is robbed by armed burglars. The show ends on a positive note, however, reminding viewers to remember the true reason for Christmas, for the Bankses find themselves much richer after the burglary than before: not in monetary terms but in love and spirit. This was just one of the many shows that touched the hearts of viewers.

The stars of *The Fresh Prince of Bel-Air* received bags of fan mail confirming that the show made a difference to many viewers. Tatyana Ali commented, "I know the show helped many teens get through difficult situations in their lives. We've touched on real problems in their lives—drug use, sex, prejudices, inner-city problems. Even if we couldn't offer them solutions, our show has shown them that they are not alone."

While *The Fresh Prince of Bel-Air* remained successful, Will Smith was soon looking to expand his acting skills. His hard work learning how to act had paid off, as he had been nominated for Golden Globe Awards for Best Actor in a TV Comedy and Best Musical Theme in 1993 and 1994 respectively, and now he wanted to make an attempt to act in movies. He received rave reviews for a role in the dramatic film *Six Degrees of Separation*, and he costarred in an action film, *Bad Boys*, with Martin Lawrence. In addition, his personal life was changing as well: he had married, had a son, and gotten divorced. It was getting harder and harder to find the "Fresh Prince" when he went before the cameras. Even though the show was still receiving good ratings, after six years Will Smith decided to move on.

"I felt like it was time to end the show," he later explained to *Ebony* magazine. "We had a nice run. . . . [T]he television show just felt confining. You're pretty much one character, and there are not many peaks and valleys, just pretty much the same old same old. And I wanted to go out while we were good. You get up to eight or nine seasons and then you're struggling. I wanted to go out solid, while we were still funny.

"When I started doing the *Fresh Prince of Bel-Air* I was 20 years old. Inside of those years I went through three careers—music, television, movies. I got married, had a baby, divorced. It's like I did a whole lot of living in that time," Will continued. "My life experiences are so far advanced beyond the character's life experiences. It was almost like a regression for me to play the character."

On May 20, 1996, after 148 episodes, the cast members of *The Fresh Prince of Bel-Air* said their final goodbyes during an emotional one-hour special. That last episode, entitled "I, Done" was a tear-jerker for the cast, crew, and viewers. The Bankses' Bel-Air home was put up for sale, and the family members decided to go their own ways. Aunt Vivian, Uncle Phil, Carlton, and Nicky planned to move to the East Coast; Hilary and Ashley decided to live in New York; Geoffrey returned to England;

and Will decided to stay in Los Angeles to finish college. This final episode was considered by many to be one of the cast's best performances, because it truly crossed over the line into real life. There was no doubt in viewers' minds that Will Smith and the cast members were upset about leaving the show, and it was obvious that many of the tears that fell and lines that were said during this episode were not simply part of the script. The humor of the episode came from Will, who did everything he could think of to prevent the house from being sold. But in the end he

After six successful years on The Fresh Prince of Bel-Air, Will decided it was time to find new challenges. The show's swan song was May 20, 1996.

admits that it is time to move on, even though it is hard to say goodbye.

Although the cast was saddened by the end of the show, all the members felt that they had created something to be proud of. The show boasted an impressive roster of guests during its six seasons, including musician B. B. King, comedian Jay Leno, actor (and former *Cosby Show* kid) Malcolm-Jamal Warner, singer/actress Vanessa Williams, rapper Queen Latifa, and talk-show host Oprah Winfrey. Will's music partner Jeff Townes also made occasional appearances on the show. Most important, the show was syndicated, meaning that it can still be seen on television in reruns.

Will Smith, on ending The Fresh Prince:

"I talked to Sherman Hemsley—George Jefferson—and he said the way that they found out that The Jeffersons was over is they came to the set one Monday and their parking spaces were gone. You know, I don't want to go out that way. They never had a final episode. You need to close that chapter in your life. I wanted to plan the going out. You know, go out standing, rather than go out on your back."

The show was not without its enemies: some critics and even civil rights activists fear that *The Fresh Prince of Bel-Air* and similar sitcoms have revived negative racial stereotypes. Sitcoms such as *The Jeffersons* and *Good Times* during the 1970s, or *Family Matters* and *Martin* in the 1990s, have all portrayed African Americans as being funny because of their characters' ridiculous antics, stupidity, and incorrect grammar and use of slang. Even physical appearance is mocked, by accentuating an actor's large ears or using exaggerated and silly facial gestures. These portrayals unnerve those who have been fighting for years to put an end to stereotypes of African Americans.

But Will Smith did not create a character who was a buffoon; he just tried to be himself. He unmasked the class clown and the family comedian to reveal a fun-loving, unique person. And while there may be some truth to the claim that black sitcom characters are stereotyped, this can be seen in nearly all television comedies, regardless of race.

Characters in hit comedy shows such as *Home Improvement*, *Seinfeld*, and *Friends* also use stereotypes to get laughs.

In any case, this criticism has not affected Will Smith's fan following. If anything, his fans have become all the more dedicated. They recall how the show paralleled their lives, producing tears as well as genuine laughs and smiles. These fans would soon get to see Will in another medium—the big screen.

6

UNEXPECTED STEPS

❧

IT IS EASY to see from his early decisions, and particularly in his move from rap artist to television actor, that Will Smith is not afraid to take risks. This trait, and the fact that many actors often attempt to move from the small screen to the big screen, made it no surprise when Will made the jump from television star to movie star. What is surprising is the way that he made this leap. Most television stars move on to Hollywood and take roles similar to the ones they portrayed on television. But most of Will's early characters were far more serious than TV's Fresh Prince.

While working on *The Fresh Prince of Bel-Air*, Will had decided he was ready to try his hand at more serious and diverse roles. Years earlier, as his rap career was taking off, Will had appeared in the 1986 film *The Imagemaker*. This movie was about a former presidential advisor who finds himself a target of death threats because of his plan to write a revealing exposé. Will played a small role as a pollster, and few of his fans were even aware that he appeared in the film. However, it could have been this small taste of the big screen that led Will to pursue film acting years later.

Will in his first role in a major movie, as Tea Cake in the 1993 Warner Brothers film Made in America.

His first real attempt at film acting, in 1992, was as a disabled boy named Manny who was confined to a wheelchair, in a low-budget independent movie called *Where the Day Takes You*. This role was nothing like Will's silly, hip-hop image from *The Fresh Prince of Bel-Air* except that Manny was also a street-smart kid. Will's first movie was dark, serious, and sad. Manny and his homeless friends, played by actors Sean Astin, Alyssa Milano, Ricki Lake, Dermot Mulroney, Balthazar Getty, and Nancy McKeon, struggle to survive in Los Angeles. Although *Where the Day Takes You* was not a big hit by any standard, it showed that Will was able to play a more serious role. This character gave him such a sense of satisfaction that it fed his desire to do more movies and explore more rounded characters.

He followed this experience with another small movie role, but this time in a bigger-budget picture with two of Hollywood's hottest stars, Ted Danson and Whoopi Goldberg. *Made in America* received considerably more publicity than *Where the Day Takes You* had. *Made in America* is about the quest of a teenaged African-American girl, played by Nia Long, to find her biological father. Her mother (played by Whoopi Goldberg) does not want her to find out that her father (Ted Danson) is a white car dealer who stars in tacky television ads. In the movie, Will plays the character Tea Cake Walters, a humorous, smooth-talking kid whose main goal is to make Nia Long his girlfriend. This role, as well as the light, comical tone of the movie, seemed to be well suited for the actor who was at that time best known as the "Fresh Prince." The story line itself allowed for bizarre and hilarious twists of fate, and the antics of Goldberg, Danson, and Smith added laughter to the script. The film was only moderately successful, but Will's small part drew the attention of critics and Hollywood executives.

After these opportunities to develop his acting skills, Will was ready to try his hand at a more substantial role. Once again, he went for a role that seemed out of character. "If you lined up one hundred

films, this would be the last one that people would expect me to do," Will admitted at the time.

The 1994 movie *Six Degrees of Separation* is based on John Guare's award-winning hit play, which was based, in part, on a true story. The film begins as a young African-American man shows up, bleeding, at the home of a wealthy Manhattan couple, Ouisa and Flan Kittredge. The young man introduces himself as Paul Poitier, the son of the famous actor Sidney Poitier, and says that he attended Harvard University with the Kittredges' children. He is bleeding,

The stars of Made in America—*Nia Long, Will Smith, Whoopi Goldberg, and Ted Danson—attend the premier of the film.*

he tells them, because he has just been mugged in Central Park.

The Kittredges invite Paul in, insist that he stay the night, and give him money to help him get home the next day. They believe Paul is a humble, intelligent, admirable person who is also the son of a well-known star, and not until they find Paul in bed with another man do the Kittredges realize that he has been lying about who he is. Paul is not really the son of Poitier but is, in fact, a homosexual con artist who is easily able to fool the Kittredges and their friends because he researched them before attempting to infiltrate their lives and win their friendship.

Will played the difficult part of Paul, which required him to switch from the smooth talker who charms the Kittredges to the con artist who takes advantage of them. The other stars of the film included Stockard Channing, who played Ouisa Kittredge, and Donald Sutherland, who portrayed Flan Kittredge.

The movie is loaded with heavy themes, as it deals with biases due to racism, class distinctions, and homosexuality. It was a difficult role for Will to attempt, but it was also a role that he knew would give him credibility as a movie actor. If he could make people see that he could be the serious, conniving Paul just as easily as he could be the fun-loving, comical Fresh Prince, then Will knew he would have other movie offers at his fingertips.

Although *Six Degrees of Separation* made just $6.41 million in its limited release, the film gained critical praise and Channing was nominated for both an Academy Award and a Golden Globe award for Best Actress. Although Will did not receive a nomination for his role as Paul, he did receive rave reviews for his performance. "Played with cheek and charisma by Smith," said one *Washington Post* staff writer. Another film reviewer commented, "The cast . . . including rap and television star Smith . . . carries off

Will's serious performance in Six Degrees of Separation *drew great praise from critics. He played the complex part of Paul, a homosexual con artist who hustles a rich New York couple played by Stockard Channing and Donald Sutherland.*

the crucial scenes of Paul's apotheosis at the Kittredge home without a hitch." *Newsweek* confirmed, "Smith, the rapper and star of TV's *Fresh Prince of Bel Air*, is an eye-opener in a complex, tricky part. Will Smith is going to be very big."

This was exactly the type of publicity that Will needed. Receiving such favorable reviews for his role as Paul confirmed for Will, his fans, and those who simply didn't believe he could play the part that he was certainly full of talent. "I guess the piece of work that I performed in that shaped me most as an actor and as a person was *Six Degrees of Separation*," Will said later. "The level of the work and the difficulty of the work helped me find out a lot about acting and about myself."

As with any diverse and complex work, an acting performance cannot escape without some negative criticism. Although Will's role as Paul offered proof that he could be a serious actor, it also sent signals to some reviewers that Will still had significant room for growth. In *Six Degrees of Separation* the script called for Will to kiss another man. Will was worrying about how this would affect his friends and family, as well as his rapper image, and he sought counsel from another African-American actor, Denzel Washington. Washington, an Oscar-winning actor, advised him against the kiss. Although Will knew that as an actor he should just play the part as it was written, he felt that he wasn't able to. Several years later, he explained his feelings to *US* magazine: "The thing that was a problem for me was my son. I had gotten myself to a yes on all other fronts. That was the only factor I couldn't shake. I was imagining what I would have said to a second grader whose father I just saw kiss a man."

The script had to be rewritten to compensate for the lack of physical contact between the actors, and Will did receive some negative reviews from critics who believed that his refusal was unprofessional and

immature. Will openly apologized later for his refusal to perform the kissing scene and acknowledged that it was an immature decision caused by his inexperience.

Despite the negative comments regarding the "kiss that never was," *Six Degrees of Separation* was a pivotal role for Will. It earned him respect in the movie industry and led to his later roles in blockbuster films. Many people believe that although films he has done since then have been far more successful financially, they have not afforded Will the same opportunity to challenge his acting abilities. James Avery, his *Fresh Prince of Bel-Air* costar, agrees. "He has a lot more talent than these films [*Bad Boys, Independence Day*] are allowing him to express,"

While Bad Boys, Will's 1995 film with Martin Lawrence, will never be considered a great movie, once again his acting was singled out for praise, and he proved that he could play an action hero.

Avery said in a 1997 *US* magazine story. "I think there's a lot more going on there than anyone knows. I think there is a lot more going on there than he really is aware of."

Will's next film, the 1995 action comedy *Bad Boys*, proved to be another turning point in his film career. Again Smith surprised fans by accepting a role substantially different from his last one. Will joined forces with another sitcom star, Martin Lawrence, to play police officers protecting a woman (Tea Leoni) who witnessed a murder. Although the movie did not get particularly good reviews—for example, *People* magazine said the film had "minus-250 points of entertainment value"—once again Will Smith was praised for his acting. The same review noted, "Smith is an actor with a refined sense of comedy. He is also physically imposing enough to pull off a serious action film."

And *Bad Boys* was a great success by the standards of the action-movie genre: it made a lot of money. The film grossed over $66 million in the United States and more than $100 million worldwide, and proved that Will Smith could draw a large audience. With his popularity and the ability he displayed in his previous effort, Will soon found himself in demand. "*Six Degrees* and *Bad Boys* were the two films that really set me up in a position to be offered all different types of movies in Hollywood," Will later acknowledged.

Looking back on Will Smith's film career is like peering through a kaleidoscope. His roles, though distinctly different, also blend together, building upon one another and each time illuminating a new dimension of Will. Even in moving from dark drama to action-packed roles, Will was able to retain his image as a comedian and entertainer. Each of his

Will Smith, on making blockbuster movies:

"I try not to pay attention to the box office. Just do the work. Enjoy it if it's a good movie, and you're happy with your work. Let that be enough. Not to have to earn $100 million in seventeen minutes. It's too much pressure, and it is really out of your control."

early movies helped to establish his acting credibility and propel him in new and exciting directions. With his next film, the monster hit *Independence Day*, Will Smith would move in a new direction—international movie star.

7

MEN IN BLACK

❧

MOST OF WILL SMITH'S film roles have been more serious than the character he played in *The Fresh Prince of Bel-Air*. Will admits that he intentionally looked for film roles that would require him to do more than just be funny. "Going into the movies I wanted to do something a little different and then maybe down the line get back into the comedies," he once explained. "Robin Williams and Tom Hanks go back and forth, but I think from watching their careers it's really important to make it clear that you can do something other than comedies."

He's proven that he can move beyond the role of comedian to be extremely successful in all facets of acting, and it is quite likely that Will's career will continue to flourish. "Will Smith is a rocket ship," says NBC Entertainment president Warren Littlefield. "He took off and just kept going." But his success is due as much to the hard work he puts into preparing for a film as it is to his talent.

When he was offered the chance to play one of the leading roles in *Independence Day*, Will Smith knew that research and careful preparation for the part of the Marine pilot would be the key to a good performance. He learned the basic skills for flying an F-16 by practicing in a flight simulator with an actual Marine lieutenant and trained with soldiers on a military base to prepare for the role of Captain Steve

Will Smith, wearing his Philadelphia Phillies baseball jersey, holds the 1998 Grammy Award that he won for Best Rap Solo Performance. He was honored for his single "Men in Black," from the film of the same name.

In Men in Black, Will and Tommy Lee Jones made an unlikely pair as super-secret government agents who protect the Earth from dangerous aliens that are already living here undetected.

Hiller. When the movie hit the theaters, it was obvious that Will's hard work had paid off in a big way, as Independence Day broke box-office records to become one of the biggest moneymaking movies of all time.

After the filming of Independence Day was complete, Will accepted a role in a Steven Spielberg film, Men in Black, and began working on the science-fiction/action movie. Because Will had always concentrated on playing diverse characters from one movie to the next, it may have seemed a little strange to some people that he would agree to play the hero of Men in Black immediately after his role in

Independence Day. But Will had many reasons to say yes to *Men in Black.* Like other actors, Will had waited for the day that Spielberg would ask him to star in one of his films. One of the most popular directors of all time, Spielberg's hits include *Jaws, Raiders of the Lost Ark, E.T., Jurassic Park, Schindler's List,* and many others. "You can't tell Steven Spielberg no," Will explained to *Ebony* magazine after Spielberg had personally called him on the phone and asked him to do this movie.

Another reason that Will was attracted to *Men in Black* was that he enjoys the science-fiction/action film genre. "Yeah, I'm really drawn to it," he said. "I like doing science fiction. I like action. I like the genre of the 'big-budget-Hollywood–blow 'em up–shoot 'em up' movies. That's for me. It's physical. You get to do stunts and all that."

The role that Will was asked to play in *Men in Black* also appealed to him. His character was a top-secret federal agent, simply referred to as Agent J, whose job was to keep an eye on aliens that lived on earth. Agent J was funny, cocky, smooth, and intelligent—characteristics that fit Will Smith perfectly. His partner, Agent K, was played by Tommy Lee Jones, who had starred in blockbuster hits such as *The Fugitive.* And there was one more reason that this role appealed to Will: it would be his largest film paycheck thus far. He reportedly received $5 million for his *Men in Black* performance.

Will enjoyed working with *Men In Black*'s director, Barry Sonnenfeld, and with his costar Tommy Lee Jones, despite Jones's reputation as a "serious" person. "We had a ball on the set of this movie," Will said in an interview with ABC's *Mr. Showbiz* website. "Tommy Lee Jones is silly, you know. He's making jokes. . . . People look at the characters Tommy plays as not having a sense of humor, but it's actually the opposite. You have to have a brilliant comedic mind to be able to do that type of straight, nothing, deadpan delivery and make it hilarious. He's a technical comedian; he has a brilliant technical understanding of comedy in a scene. We called it 'soft pitching.' . . . Just lobbing those jokes up there for me."

The story line of *Men in Black* creates a different mood than that of *Independence Day*. The dreadful fear of an alien invasion is replaced by quirky comedy about members of a top-secret government agency that monitors aliens who have taken up residence here on Earth. The agents, nicknamed "men in black" because of their dark suits and sunglasses, must protect Earth from an intergalactic war while keeping other humans unaware that extraterrestrials are living in their midst. The plot is simple, but the dialogue and the special effects create excellent entertainment. Many critics found the movie to be powerful and effective. "*Men in Black* is the wryest, sharpest, most entertaining special effects film in recent memory. . . . To say that the film doesn't take itself seriously is missing the point. It doesn't take anything seriously, not you, not me, not even Tommy Lee Jones," one surprised reviewer said. Another reviewer commented on the movie's place among other summer blockbuster films: "Too many big-studio movies this summer begin with guns blazing and vehicles crashing before the opening credits have even rolled. *Men in Black* begins with a splat: a firefly wings its way from outer space to Earth only to encounter, with fatal results, a windshield. It's a witty and inventive opening, and indicative of what's to come in this delightfully droll, off-beat sci-fi comedy."

Men in Black did not break the sales records that *Independence Day* set, but it did extremely well at the box office, becoming the number one film of 1997 and racking up $250 million in ticket sales. *Men in Black*'s popularity continued with strong video sales when the movie arrived in stores just in time for the 1997 holiday season.

In addition to Will's acting in *Men in Black*, he

returned to his musical roots to create the movie's title song and several others for the film's soundtrack. The catchy single remained high on the charts long after the movie left the theaters, and the video of the song won MTV's Best Video from a Film award. The line dance that Will performs in the music video with some of the movie's aliens made its way onto club dance floors across the nation. The *Men in Black* soundtrack won the award for Favorite Soundtrack at the 25th Annual American Music Awards in January 1998, and in February of that year Will won his third Grammy Award for the single "Men in Black." Appearing to perform his hit song wearing a Philadelphia Phillies baseball jersey, Will later recalled winning his first Grammy, in 1989, when he boycotted the ceremony because the rap awards were not considered important enough to be televised.

In the years following the release of DJ Jazzy Jeff

Agent J (Will) holds a new-born alien. The special effects, along with Will's humorous performance, made Men in Black *"the wryest, sharpest, most entertaining special effects film in recent memory," according to one reviewer.*

and the Fresh Prince's last album, *Code Red*, in 1993, Will Smith had told interviewers that he would not be returning to music because he wanted to focus on making movies. While Will's career was taking off, Jeff Townes had kept a low profile. He did appear several times as a friend of Will's on *The Fresh Prince of Bel-Air*, but he was devoting more of his time to producing albums for his company, A Touch of Jazz.

But in November of 1997, Will contradicted his earlier statement by releasing his first solo album, *Big Willie Style*. He maintained his ties with "Jazzy" Jeff, who produced several songs on the album. Will also worked with other well-known hip-hop musicians and producers, including Trackmaster, Poke and Tone, and Warren G. Sauce, in making this album, his first in four years.

Will's fans were thrilled at his return to music, and the first single from the 16-track album, "Gettin' Jiggy Wit It," hit number one on the Billboard singles chart in March 1998. Reviewers also liked the album. "[*Big Willie Style*] crackles with the lucid energy of early-'80s rap hits. . . . he displays the confident craft of a screenwriter and the unthreatened bounce of a guy with little to prove. . . . an exceptional megacelebrity album," said *Rolling Stone*, while a reviewer in *Vibe* wrote, "The saving grace of the former Fresh Prince is that, as an MC, he's never taken himself too seriously. . . . *Big Willie Style*'s wisecracking, fun-filled material is expected—and fun to digest."

Will Smith, on what "Jiggy" means:

"Jiggy is the next level beyond cool. Jiggy is when you're cool times 10, like in the 50s, the Fonz woulda been Jiggy. Some people are cool, some people are kinda hot. Some people are kinda sexy. Some people mix all that in one. Not many people can reach that plateau that we call Jiggy-ness."

Fans who had wondered why it took Will so long to record another album got their answer during an interview he gave with television's *Access Hollywood*. Will admitted that he had lost confidence in his ability to produce great hits. After the phenomenal success of *He's the DJ, I'm the Rapper* in 1988, the sales of

his follow-up albums had steadily declined. His confidence was also shaken when people continually told him that he couldn't be both "King of Hollywood" and "Prince" of the music industry. But with his success, Will has settled on a simple response: "I'll be the first to break down those doors."

During another interview, he gave some good advice to a young fan on how to make a career in hip-hop: "You've got to love hip-hop and not money. You've gotta do it 'cause it's something that you love from the heart and not something about getting paid. And if you keep doing it—and if you keep loving it—then you can't help but be successful."

However, Will Smith will probably focus on movies, rather than music, in the near future. In

Men in Black blasted to the top of the list of the most popular films for 1997—Will's second summer blockbuster in two years.

December of 1997 he worked on a film called *Enemy of the State*, which will also star Gene Hackman and Jon Voight. The director is Tony Scott, who made the huge hit *Top Gun* in the 1980s. And in April 1998 he started filming *The Wild, Wild West*, which is based on a 1960s television program. Will and director Barry Sonnefeld were reunited on this project.

There has also been some discussion of movie sequels to Will's blockbusters—*Bad Boys*, *Independence Day*, and *Men in Black*—but nothing has been finalized yet. "We're looking at possibly doing [*Bad Boys II*] next year but we're in the process of getting a script together," Will told fans that tuned in to chat with him on America Online's Hub Music in December of 1997. "In order for me to make a sequel for any movie that I've ever made, it's gotta be better than the first one."

Will has also recently tried his hand at writing. In 1997 he and his wife, movie star Jada Pinkett, wrote a film script together for a romantic comedy called *Love for Hire*. Universal Pictures purchased the script, and Will plans to act in the movie. Pinkett will not appear in the film, and the couple has told interviewers that they have no plans to make a movie together. "You don't want to put that kind of strain on your relationship," Will told *US* magazine.

Will's name has also been linked to several projects that are reportedly in the works. In addition to *Love for Hire*, Will has expressed interest in a movie being made by African-American filmmaker Spike Lee titled *Clutch City*, about the 1994–95 Houston Rockets. Other actors who are being considered for the project include John Travolta and Damon Wayans. In March 1998, Universal Pictures announced that Will would team up with another musician-turned-actor, Whitney Houston, in *Anything for Love*, a film about a man who dumps his girlfriend only to realize eight months later that he's made a terrible mistake. Will is also interested in a role in

Irwin Winkler's adaptation of the critically acclaimed book *Lush Life: A Biography of Billy Strayhorn*. Oscar-winner Denzel Washington will also star in this movie about 1920s jazz pianist and composer Billy Strayhorn, which is expected to be released in 1998.

Will takes his position as a role model seriously, and that affects the choices he makes in his career—from deciding not to kiss Anthony Michael Hall in *Six Degrees of Separation* to the roles that he will take in the future. "I want to play positive characters. I want to play characters that represent really strong, positive black images," Will stated in a 1996 interview. "So that's the thing I consider when I'm taking a role after I decide if it's something that I want to do. At this point, I don't want to play a gangster, unless it's a role that has a different or more positive message."

While fans may wonder when the next Will Smith blockbuster film will hit theaters, or what it will be about, after the release of *Men in Black* Will joked, "It's just my job to save the world every summer. . . . I really don't know what I'm going to do for an encore next year. But it has to be something big on the July 4 weekend." In the meantime, he has quite a few things in his personal life to keep him happily occupied.

8

FAMILY COMES FIRST

❧

DESPITE THE FAME that Will has enjoyed as a result of his professional career, he realizes that remaining successful professionally will require strong character and solid values in his personal life. Three of the most important roles in Will's life have nothing to do with films or television. They are the roles of father, husband, and son.

Although Will's parents did not encourage his rapping career when he was in high school, they did support their son when he decided to focus on a career in music. Perhaps that is why his family remains a top priority for Will, and he makes an effort to remain close to them. In fact, his siblings all work for Will: his brother Harry is Will's chief financial officer; sister Ellen is the receptionist in his office; and his older sister Pam helps to manage his businesses in Philadelphia.

Although on television and in movies Will has often played a smooth talker who has a way with lovely ladies, he doesn't feel that he has ever been a "ladies' man." In *Will Power!*, Will is quoted as saying, "I've always been a one-girl guy. . . . I've never been out there trying to find a different girl every night." His desire to remain true to himself and to others is the force that guides even his love life.

Will has had three lengthy relationships. He met his first love, Tanya Moore, in 1989 while performing

Will Smith, holding his son Trey, and his girlfriend Jada Pinkett attend the Los Angeles premier of Independence Day *in 1996. In December of 1997 Will and Jada married.*

at San Diego State University. Tanya, a business major, was 19 when she and Will began dating. At the time, Will was gaining popularity as a rapper, earning a lot of money and spending it even faster. Tanya was a significant part of Will's life during those years, and she stayed with him after his money crisis, helping him rebuild his life and get his career back on track. No one knows what went wrong with their relationship, but their breakup came as a surprise to everyone who knew the couple.

After his relationship with Tanya ended, Will fell madly in love with a fashion design student, Sheree Zampino. They met while visiting a mutual friend on the set of the television show *A Different World* in 1991. For Will it was love at first sight, but Sheree needed to be won over by "princely" charm before agreeing to a date. The two began a friendship that slowly became a loving relationship. Once they began dating it did not take long for their relationship to become serious. In just a few months Will decided to propose. On Christmas Eve in 1991, Will told Sheree that he was flying back to Philadelphia to spend the holidays with his family; instead he surprised her by getting on his knees and offering her a diamond ring.

Sheree and Will married on May 9, 1992. Many friends and family witnessed the vows they exchanged that day, including Jeff Townes, Denzel Washington, and Magic Johnson. The two seemed to be a perfect match—Sheree's quick wit was a perfect complement to Will's humor, and they enjoyed one another's company immensely.

In late fall of that year, Sheree and Will had a son, Willard C. Smith III. From that day forward, Will's focus was on his son, whom he nicknamed Trey. Will constantly showered Trey with love and affection. Will later described becoming a father as an extremely spiritual experience because he felt as though God had given him the most beautiful gift he had ever

received. "When the doctor handed him to me, I realized things were different now," Will recalled.

Will takes parenting very seriously and has attempted to instill in Trey the same discipline and respect that his parents taught him. By all accounts, he has succeeded so far. Trey often visited the set of *The Fresh Prince of Bel-Air*, and members of the cast and crew have commented on how well-mannered he was. Alfonso Ribeiro recalled Trey's politeness. "If Trey wanted something, he'd ask, 'Excuse me, can I play with this?,'" he told *People*. "He knew about the bell that went off when we started taping. When he heard it, Trey would put his finger to his mouth and say 'Shhhhh!'"

Will hopes to continue to guide Trey toward this type of positive behavior. "There's three things that

Will and Jeff Goldblum accepted a 1997 Kid's Choice Award for Independence Day, *which was named "favorite movie."*

Will and his first wife, Sheree Zampino, were married for four years. The couple had a child together, Willard Smith III, nicknamed Trey.

you can give your child," Smith told *US* magazine. "You give them love, you give them knowledge, you give them discipline. You give your kids those three things, and everything else is in the hands of the Lord." When Trey is older, Will says, he would like to teach him how to play two of his own favorite games: chess and golf. "They teach you self-control and patience," Smith explained. "If you allow your passion to take you over and have its way with you, you can't win."

The importance of fatherhood to Will is revealed in one of the singles off his album *Big Willie Style*. The song "Just the Two of Us" is dedicated to his son, and it allows Will's listeners to understand Trey's role in his father's life.

That was one reason it was so difficult when Will and Sheree decided to divorce in 1995. The couple never publicly discussed the reason for the separation, with Will often responding in vague, indirect terms. "We had a son, and my career was taking off. There was a lot of pressure that didn't allow the marriage to blossom," he told *People* shortly after the separation. Later Will told an interviewer from *US* magazine, "I had no business getting married. Neither one of us was ready. We hadn't experienced enough life yet to be together."

However, the star admits that it was Sheree's idea to end the marriage, not his. Will believed that when he got married it would last forever, and he feared that a divorce would hurt their son. "That was a very difficult period in my life. A lot of pain," Will told *US* magazine. However, Will and Sheree have remained respectful of one another since the divorce, and they share custody of Trey.

It was after this failed relationship that Will fell in love with Jada Pinkett, a well-known actress who has appeared in such films as *Menace II Society*, *The Inkwell*, *A Low Down Dirty Shame*, and the block-buster hit *The Nutty Professor* with comedian Eddie Murphy.

Will and Jada had actually met in 1990 during the first season of *The Fresh Prince of Bel-Air*. Jada had auditioned for the role of Will's girlfriend, but the show's producers did not give her the part because they believed she was too short. However,

Will attended the Million Man March, a civil rights march organized in October 1995. He later called the gathering of hundreds of thousands of African-American men one of the most spiritual events in his life.

Will and Jada remained friends. They found their relationship evolving after Will's failed marriage and after Jada broke up with her boyfriend. "I helped him understand what happened in his marriage . . . and he helped me see what happened in my relationship. He's become my best friend. There's nothing I can't say to him, nothing I can't share," she told *People* in 1996. Will agrees: "Jada Pinkett is my best friend, and when you can combine your best friend in the world with the person who is also your lover and your partner, that is an emotional and spiritual and physical ecstasy that is unmatched. Basically, she's cool."

The couple assured the media that they had no

wedding plans through the summer and fall of 1997. "There's no reason to rush into anything," Will said in the August 1997 issue of US magazine. "We are very much in love and life is just so beautiful. We haven't really talked about [marriage]." Nonetheless, Jada and Will were married on December 31, 1997, in Baltimore, Maryland. Although they were only engaged briefly, their wedding was an extravagant event costing over $3 million.

One strength of Will and Jada's marriage is that its foundation rests on the fact that both individuals are members of the acting profession and, therefore, better able to understand the demands often placed on actors. While this doesn't guarantee that their relationship will always be perfect, it cushions the pressures of a stressful career, one that often separates couples. Will and Jada had their first child, a boy named Jaden Christopher Syre Smith, on July 8, 1998. Will is looking forward to having a family with Jada, and admits that although he remains close to Trey, he still feels sad that he cannot see his son all the time:

> Actually, I think [Sheree] did me a favor. But I'm hugely family oriented. To me, a child being able to hear the thunder outside and to run and jump into bed with his mother and father—I remember that from Philly. That's a memory my son will never have. For me, I can't imagine life being any better than it is for me. Jada is my soul mate. But there's still a pain that I feel, that my son will never experience some of the beauty that I experienced of having a family. There's almost a kind of weird guilt for my extreme happiness.

With his son, his new wife, and his career, Will is both happy and busy. He finds it difficult at times to accomplish all that he would like, but he believes that people just need to take time out to enjoy life. One of Will's favorite ways to relax is by playing golf. He has his own private golf hole on the property around his home, so he is able to pick up a club and

Will, Jada, and Trey at the premier of Men in Black *in 1997. As Will's career continues to soar, he hopes to remain grounded by putting his family first.*

take a swing whenever he likes, which is practically every day. Will also enjoys the company of Indo and Zahki, his two Rottweiler dogs.

Although Will has become a big star, he is still affected by the problems that all African Americans face in the United States. There have been times when he's been stopped by a police officer who assumed he was a thief because he was a young black man who happened to be driving a nice car. He later turned that incident into an episode of *The Fresh Prince of Bel-Air* in which Will and Carlton are pulled over when driving Judge Banks's luxury automobile through a nice neighborhood. "I've been punched in the face and kicked by police," he told interviewer Chris Heath in 1997. "Fill out a report and internal affairs will come back and say, basically, what you said didn't happen. All through your life growing up as a young black man you see that happen to everybody around you.

"Probably from the time that you can understand race, 7 or 8 years old, there's a weight that you carry," he continued. "If a white person gets into a fight with a black guy, he feels safer when the cops come. For the black guy, now you're really scared, because you've won the first fight, but now there's a guy with a gun and a nightstick."

Will definitely believes that racism exists in Hollywood, as in other aspects of life in the United States. "It's a part of living in our world and it's something that, unfortunately, we all have to deal with," he said. "I think it's a cancer that erodes the very base of our existence." In October 1996, Will joined hundreds of thousands of other African Americans in a rally in Washington, D.C. The Million Man March, organized by Nation of Islam leader Louis Farrakhan, was meant to be a day of renewed spirituality for black Americans. It was an important day for Will Smith, who said that, next to the birth of his son, "the most spiritual event in [my] life was attending the Million Man March. . . . [It] was the only time in my life I ever felt safe."

Will believes that the schools he attended growing up allowed him to better understand both white and black people. "[I had] the best cross section that anybody could have," he reflected. "The first eight years of schooling was with all white people, so that helped me to understand how white people think. I think that transition is what helped me bridge the gap, because that's what my success has really been about: bridging the gap between the black community and the white community." Will wants all cultures, races, and religions to be able to enjoy his acting and his other talents, and it is obvious from the diversity of his fans that his wish is coming true. Why has Will been so successful? He says the answer is simple: "I enjoy life, I enjoy people. And people—black, white, Asian, or alien—enjoy that energy."

Because of his success, and because he is thankful for everything that he has, Will enjoys helping others, especially kids, whenever he has an opportunity. He has become involved in many children's charities and fundraisers. "It feels good to be here with these kids," Will said during one visit to an orphanage, the McLaren Children's Center, a couple of years ago. "There are a lot of smiles here today. It's real easy to make their day. As a celebrity, it's easy to forget how important it is to help out. I want to encourage others to do it." Will has also served as the master of ceremonies for the NBA Stay in School Jam, an event that encourages kids to continue their educations.

Will Smith, on Will Smith:

"I like to have fun. I like to be silly, make jokes, and people enjoy that. People generally have fun in my life. So when the camera's turned on I'm having fun, and I think people can see that, people can feel that when they watch the movie."

It is because of social involvement of this nature that Will has earned respect for who he is along with his popularity as a movie, television, and music star. Fans adore him because he is sincere, generous, and sensitive, and he has retained many of the traditional values that he was taught growing up in Philadelphia. But even with the label "the nicest guy in Hollywood," Will has earned his place among Tinseltown's power brokers. In *Entertainment Weekly*'s 1997 "Power Issue," which rates the 101 most powerful people in Hollywood, Will Smith ranked 44th. The majority of the 43 people ahead of him were producers, directors, or studio presidents, so Will was actually one of the top-rated actors, along with such superstars as Jerry Seinfeld, Tom Cruise, Harrison Ford, Mel Gibson, Tom Hanks, John Travolta, Jim Carrey, Clint Eastwood, and Rosie O'Donnell—a pretty impressive group by any standard.

But even if his career falters, Will Smith is not concerned. "Hollywood's a tough town. I look at it like, you're driving on the highway and it's raining, and there's that one car broken down on the side of the road. Hundreds of thousands of cars in perfect working order in every direction, and there's that one car. . . . One day, you're going to be that car broken down on the side of the road. And when you are, it's cool, it's okay. Tow truck's gonna come. You're gonna get it fixed, you're gonna be back on the road. You just gotta ride through it."

Will tries not to spend a lot of time worrying over how things will turn out or fretting over past mistakes. He has never been afraid to be himself, and those who know him believe this is one aspect of Will Smith that even the greatest success won't alter. No matter what course his future may take, the unique qualities that compose Will Smith can be found in the lyrics he raps, in the characters he portrays, and especially in his roles as father, husband, and family man.

CHRONOLOGY

—— ❧ ——

1968	Born Willard Smith Jr. on September 25 in Philadelphia, Pennsylvania
1986	Forms the rap duo DJ Jazzy Jeff and The Fresh Prince with Jeff Townes; graduates from Overbrook High School; releases first single, "Girls Ain't Nothing but Trouble"; makes film debut with a minor role in *The Imagemaker*
1987	Releases first album, *Rock the House*
1988	Releases second album, *He's the DJ, I'm the Rapper,* which goes triple platinum
1989	Wins American Music Awards for Best Album and Best Artist in the rap category; "Parents Just Don't Understand" wins Grammy Award for Best Rap Single; releases *And in This Corner*
1990	Pilot episode of *The Fresh Prince of Bel-Air* airs on September 10
1991	Releases album *Homebase*; wins Grammy Award for "Summertime"; wins Nickelodeon Kids' Choice Award as Favorite TV Actor
1992	Wins NAACP Image Award for Outstanding Rap Artist; appears in the film *Where the Day Takes You*; marries Sheree Zampino; son Willard C. "Trey" Smith III is born
1993	Releases *Code Red*; works with stars Whoopi Goldberg and Ted Danson in *Made in America*; *The Fresh Prince of Bel-Air* is nominated for a Golden Globe Award as Best TV Comedy
1994	Nominated for a Golden Globe Award as Best Musical Actor for *The Fresh Prince of Bel-Air*; gains recognition for his performance in *Six Degrees of Separation*
1995	Costars with comedian Martin Lawrence in *Bad Boys*, for which he receives a NATO/ShoWest Award; divorces Sheree Zampino
1996	Final episode of *The Fresh Prince of Bel-Air* airs on May 20; stars in blockbuster film *Independence Day*
1997	Costars in summer blockbuster *Men in Black*; Wins MTV's Best Video from a Film Award; releases first solo album, *Big Willie Style*; marries actress Jada Pinkett on New Year's Eve
1998	Wins Grammy Award for Best Rap Single for the title song from the *Men in Black* soundtrack; "Gettin' Jiggy Wit It" reaches number one on Billboard chart; son Jaden Christopher Syre Smith is born

BIBLIOGRAPHY

"Alien Invasion!" *Newsweek*, 8 July 1996.

Berenson, Jan. *Will Power! A Biography of Will Smith*. New York: Pocket Books, 1997.

Cerio, Gregory. "Mr. Smith Goes to Stardom." *People Weekly*, August 1996.

Dolan, Sean. *Pursuing the Dream*. New York: Chelsea House Publishers, 1995.

Heath, Chris. "Will Smith." *US* 235 August 1997.

Norment, Lynn. "Will Smith." *Ebony*, August 1996.

Samuels, Allison, and Karen Schoemer. "Box Office Prince." *Newsweek*, 22 July 1996.

Wolcott, James. "Reborn on the Fourth of July." *The New Yorker*, 15 July 1996.

DISCOGRAPHY & FILMOGRAPHY

DISCOGRAPHY

As DJ Jazzy Jeff and the Fresh Prince
  1987: *Rock the House*
  1988: *He's the D.J, I'm the Rapper*
  1989: *And in This Corner . . .*
  1991: *Homebase*
  1993: *Code Red*

Solo albums
  1997: *Big Willie Style*

FILMOGRAPHY

1986: *The Imagemaker*
1992: *Where the Day Takes You*
1993: *Made in America*
1994: *Six Degrees of Separation*
1995: *Bad Boys*
1996: *Independence Day*
1997: *Men in Black*

INDEX

PICTURE CREDITS

STACEY STAUFFER has a degree in English and a concentration in creative writing from Ursinus College in Collegeville, Pennsylvania. Several of her poems and short stories have been published in literary magazines and her articles have appeared in various publications, including the *Chester County Press* and a multicultural newspaper, *La Voz*. She has worked as a journalist, freelance writer, and editor.

NATHAN IRVIN HUGGINS, one of America's leading scholars in the field of black studies, helped select the titles for the BLACK AMERICANS OF ACHIEVEMENT series, for which he also served as senior consulting editor. He was the W. E. B. DuBois Professor of History and Afro-American Studies at Harvard University and the director of the W. E. B. DuBois Institute for Afro-American Research at Harvard. He received his doctorate from Harvard in 1962 and returned there as professor in 1980 after teaching at Columbia University, the University of Massachusetts, Lake Forest College, and the California State University, Long Beach. He was the author of four books and dozens of articles, including *Black Odyssey: The Afro-American Ordeal in Slavery*, *The Harlem Renaissance*, and *Slave and Citizen: The Life of Frederick Douglass*, and was associated with the Children's Television Workshop, National Public Radio, the Boston Athenaeum, the Museum of Afro-American History, the Howard Thurman Educational Trust, and Upward Bound. Professor Huggins died in 1989, at the age of 62, in Cambridge, Massachusetts.